Index

Deal 1

When I discovered the joy of Bridge (as a teenager), it was the ability to extract an extra trick from a seemingly hopeless situation, a little like magic, that intrigued me most. My mission in this book is to simplify the techniques involved, making them more accessible to you.

The definition of the word "Endplay" in the Official Encyclopaedia is somewhat woolly: "A play taking place usually towards the end of the hand, though sometimes earlier."
There are three basic types of endplay:

(A). The Throw-in. Putting the opposition on play where every lead they next make helps you.

(B). The Trump Coup. Any endplay revolving around trumps.

(C). The Squeeze. Putting the opposition under pressure, such that any discard is fatal.

Take a suit such as AJ2 facing K103. If you as declarer play this suit, you have to guess which opponent holds the queen in order to take all three tricks (leading low to the jack, or low to the ten, as appropriate). However if an opponent leads the suit, then the queen is picked up for you and you must score all three tricks.

Your mission with such a suit is to organise the play such that your put an opponent on play (the "throw-in") at a point where they have no better alternative but to lead the key suit. You will therefore needed to "eliminate" all their better alternatives first.

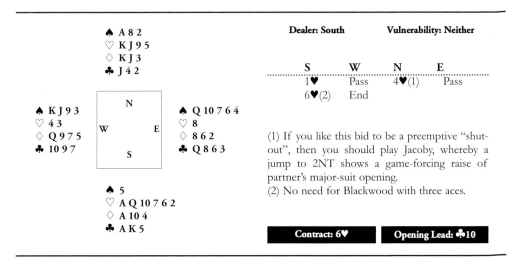

Dealer: South   Vulnerability: Neither

S	W	N	E
1♥	Pass	4♥(1)	Pass
6♥(2)	End		

(1) If you like this bid to be a preemptive "shut-out", then you should play Jacoby, whereby a jump to 2NT shows a game-forcing raise of partner's major-suit opening.
(2) No need for Blackwood with three aces.

Contract: 6♥   Opening Lead: ♣10

Our first deal features just such an "Elimination and Throw-in". Covering the ten of clubs with dummy's jack, East (as expected) in turn covers with the queen, and you win the king. You have a certain club loser and appear to be guessing the queen of diamonds for your slam.

Not so. Draw trumps, then eliminate spades by crossing to the ace, ruffing a spade, crossing to a third trump, ruffing the last spade. Now play ace and a third club.

Whichever opponent wins the club is endplayed. They must either lead a black card, enabling you to trump in one hand and discard a diamond from the other; or lead a diamond to resolve the guess for you. 12 tricks and slam made.

Deal 2

The trigger for adopting an Elimination and Throw-in, as declarer, is a suit you would like the opponents to lead.

Here are some examples:

KJ2	J32	K92
facing	facing	facing
A103	Q54	Q103

In order to force the opponents to lead the key suit, you must first eliminate all their better (i.e. safer) options. Take this six-card ending with hearts trumps - are the conditions right for a Throw-in?

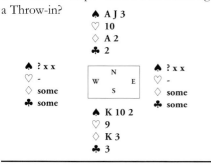

♠ A J 3
♡ 10
◇ A 2
♣ 2

♠ ? x x
♡ -
◇ some
♣ some

N
W   E
S

♠ ? x x
♡ -
◇ some
♣ some

♠ K 10 2
♡ 9
◇ K 3
♣ 3

You have many of the necessary ingredients: a suit you would rather the opponents led (spades), an "exit card" (the club), plus trumps in both hands. But if you throw the opponents in with a club now, they can win and safely lead a diamond, giving you nothing and forcing you to guess the location of the queen of spades.

First you must "eliminate" diamonds, simply by cashing the ace-king. Now the lead of a club forces the opponents either to lead a spade, resolving your guess, or a minor-suit card, allowing you to trump (ruff) in one hand and discard a spade from the other: the "ruff-and-discard".

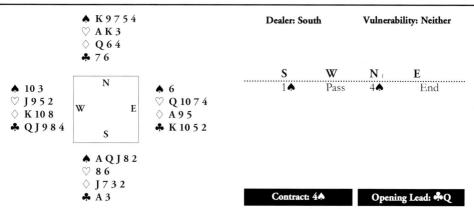

♠ K 9 7 5 4
♡ A K 3
◇ Q 6 4
♣ 7 6

♠ 10 3
♡ J 9 5 2
◇ K 10 8
♣ Q J 9 8 4

N
W   E
S

♠ 6
♡ Q 10 7 4
◇ A 9 5
♣ K 10 5 2

♠ A Q J 8 2
♡ 8 6
◇ J 7 3 2
♣ A 3

Dealer: South   **Vulnerability: Neither**

S	W	N	E
1♠	Pass	4♠	End

Contract: 4♠	Opening Lead: ♣Q

Look at the diamond suit on our featured deal. Play diamonds yourself and, provided the opponent playing second goes low on a low card, but covers an honour with their higher honour, you are bound to lose three tricks. Plus the club. Down one.

However if you can force the opponents to lead diamonds, then, by playing second-hand low, you will make a third-round trick. To execute this, you must throw them in with your

club loser having eliminated their safe options.

Win the club lead, draw trumps, then, crucially, eliminate hearts by cashing the ace-king and ruffing a heart. Now exit with the club. Whichever opponent wins is forced to lead a club/heart and give a ruff-and-discard (you will throw a diamond from dummy and ruff in hand); or lead a diamond, thereby restricting your losers to two. 10 tricks and game made.

Deal 3

The trigger for an Elimination and Throw-in is a suit you would rather the opponents lead. The key ingredients are:

(1) Trumps in both hands - or the opponents can lead a suit in which you are void in both hands, and you will have gained nothing.

(2) No suit that the opponents can lead safely.

(3) An exit card - to enable the throw-in to take place.

Tying in with the above, the process involved is:

(A) Draw trumps, leaving trumps in both hands.

(B) "Eliminate" all safe options.

(C) Play the exit card to execute the Throw in.

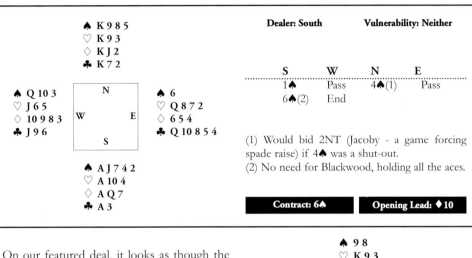

```
              ♠ K 9 8 5
              ♡ K 9 3
              ◇ K J 2
              ♣ K 7 2
♠ Q 10 3          N          ♠ 6
♡ J 6 5                      ♡ Q 8 7 2
◇ 10 9 8 3   W       E       ◇ 6 5 4
♣ J 9 6                      ♣ Q 10 8 5 4
                  S
              ♠ A J 7 4 2
              ♡ A 10 4
              ◇ A Q 7
              ♣ A 3
```

Dealer: South   Vulnerability: Neither

S	W	N	E
1♠	Pass	4♠(1)	Pass
6♠(2)	End		

(1) Would bid 2NT (Jacoby - a game forcing spade raise) if 4♠ was a shut-out.

(2) No need for Blackwood, holding all the aces.

| Contract: 6♠ | Opening Lead: ◆ 10 |

On our featured deal, it looks as though the slam depends purely on avoiding a trump loser - for surely there is a third-round heart loser. Declarer won the ten of diamonds lead, crossed to the king of trumps (preserving his finesse positions in hand), then led a second trump.

Disappointed to see East discard on the second trump, declarer rose with the ace, and was staring down one in the face. Or was he? One silver lining to the cloudy trump split was that he now had an exit card - a third trump.

First declarer needed to eliminate all West's safe exits - in clubs and diamonds. He cashed the ace of clubs, crossed to the king, and ruffed a third club. He followed by cashing the two remaining top diamonds, and now the scene was set (see five-card ending, across):

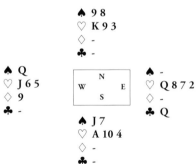

```
              ♠ 9 8
              ♡ K 9 3
              ◇ -
              ♣ -
♠ Q               N          ♠ -
♡ J 6 5       W       E      ♡ Q 8 7 2
◇ 9                          ◇ -
♣ -               S          ♣ Q
              ♠ J 7
              ♡ A 10 4
              ◇ -
              ♣ -
```

Declarer exited with the third trump and West was endplayed. A diamond would give ruff-and-discard, enabling a ruff in one hand and a heart discard from the other. So West had to broach hearts. His choice of ♥5* went ♥3, ♥Q, ♥A, and declarer could now finesse dummy's nine and so avoid a loser. 12 tricks and slam made.

*♥J works no better. Declarer rises with ♥K then finesses ♥10.

Deal 4

In your quest to make an extra trick using Elimination and Throw-in technique, sometimes you need one specific opponent to win the lead, rather than the other. Take this layout of the key suit:

	Dummy	
West	32	East
?		?
	Declarer	
	AQ	

Only from West will the lead of this suit be to your advantage. If East leads the suit, crucially through your ace-queen, you have gained nothing (and must take the same finesse you could have taken yourself, by leading from dummy to your queen). If West leads the suit, however, your queen is promoted, regardless of the whereabouts of the king.

So, in such a situation, how can you make sure that it is West you put on lead, rather than East?

Take these exit-card suits:

(A)	Dummy	
West	AJ	East
K led		
	Declarer	
	32	

You win the ace and know that West, marked with the queen, must win the second-round exit.

(B)	Dummy	
West	Q9	East
J led		
	Declarer	
	A2	

Cover West's jack with the queen; say East in turn plays the king; you win the ace, but know that West holds the ten. It will be he who wins the second-round exit-card.

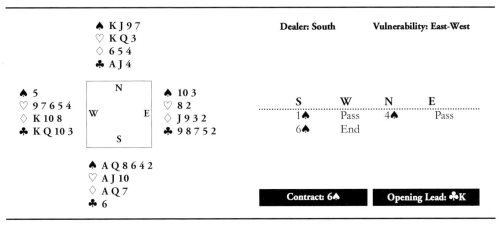

	♠ K J 9 7	
	♡ K Q 3	
	◇ 6 5 4	
	♣ A J 4	

♠ 5		♠ 10 3
♡ 9 7 6 5 4	N	♡ 8 2
◇ K 10 8	W E	◇ J 9 3 2
♣ K Q 10 3	S	♣ 9 8 7 5 2

	♠ A Q 8 6 4 2	
	♡ A J 10	
	◇ A Q 7	
	♣ 6	

Dealer: South   **Vulnerability: East-West**

S	W	N	E
1♠	Pass	4♠	Pass
6♠	End		

Contract: 6♠   **Opening Lead: ♣K**

Some fancy-footwork was needed by declarer to throw specifically West in. For a diamond lead (around to the ace-queen) would only be helpful from West.

Winning the king of clubs lead with the ace, you seek to avoid the diamond finesse. Clearly you must draw trumps and eliminate hearts; if you also ruff both clubs to eliminate that suit, and plan to lead a diamond from dummy, all will be well if East follows low. You can then insert the seven to endplay West into giving a ruff-and-discard or leading a diamond around to your ace-queen. But an alert East will foil this plan by inserting the nine or jack of diamonds.

The solution is to draw trumps, ruff the low club, eliminate hearts finishing in dummy, then lead the jack of clubs, discarding your low diamond (key play). West, known to have the queen, wins, but must now lead a diamond. A neat Loser-on-Loser play.

Deal 5

The three basic ingredients for an Elimination and Throw-in are:

(A) *Opposing trumps drawn, with trumps in both hands.*

(B) *No suit the opponents can lead safely.*

(C) *An exit-card.*

Let us consider point (A). Having trumps in both your hand and dummy is essential for the Throw-in; otherwise you cannot take advantage of the opponents exiting in a suit in which you are void in both hands - the ruff-and-discard. However sometimes you cannot afford to draw all the opposing trumps (if to do so will remove all of dummy's trumps).

All is not lost. You must leave trump(s) out in the one opponent's hand, and try to throw in the other opponent. Take this deal.

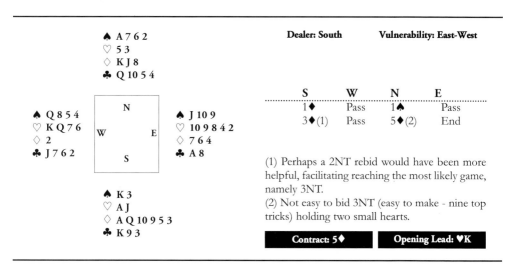

Dealer: South   Vulnerability: East-West

S	W	N	E
1♦	Pass	1♠	Pass
3♦(1)	Pass	5♦(2)	End

(1) Perhaps a 2NT rebid would have been more helpful, facilitating reaching the most likely game, namely 3NT.

(2) Not easy to bid 3NT (easy to make - nine top tricks) holding two small hearts.

Contract: 5♦   **Opening Lead: ♥K**

Declarer beat West's king of hearts with the ace, and made a mental note that it would be West who won the second heart (known to hold the queen). Declarer's problem was the jack of clubs. If he had to play the suit himself, he would be guessing its whereabouts, but if an opponent led a club, the guess would be resolved and only the ace be lost.

Planning a Throw-in, declarer needed to draw trumps and eliminate spades, currently a safe exit. He could then throw West in with his queen of hearts.

Short of dummy entries, declarer immediately cashed the king of spades, crossed to the ace, and ruffed a third spade (high). He crossed to a trump and ruffed a fourth spade (East throwing a heart). He then led a second trump, hoping both opponents would follow. If so, he would have a perfect Elimination and Throw-in. As it was, West discarded on the second trump.

Ostensibly this was bad news - East still had a trump. But because declarer knew that it would be West winning the exit card, he could cope with it.

Leaving East's trump outstanding (as he needed dummy to have a trump), declarer exited with a heart. If West led a third heart, he could ruff in dummy, whilst discarding a club from hand; and if West led a club his problems in the suit would be solved.

11 tricks and game made - using "Partial Elimination" technique.

Deal 6

Sometimes a perfect Elimination and Throw-in cannot be achieved. Last deal we saw an opposing trump having to be left out, but declarer was still able to bring off the desired ending.

This deal we consider another imperfection: all the suits cannot be eliminated, so that one opponent has a safe exit. Don't despair. Provided you throw in the other opponent, your strategy will still work. Take this "Partial Elimination"

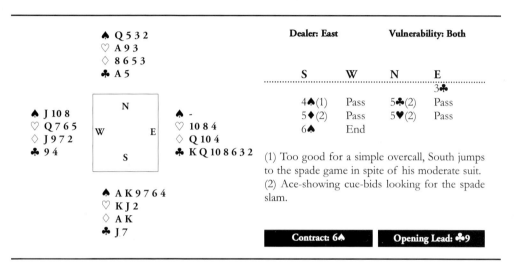

♠ Q 5 3 2
♡ A 9 3
◇ 8 6 5 3
♣ A 5

♠ J 10 8   N   ♠ -
♡ Q 7 6 5   W   E   ♡ 10 8 4
◇ J 9 7 2   ◇ Q 10 4
♣ 9 4   S   ♣ K Q 10 8 6 3 2

♠ A K 9 7 6 4
♡ K J 2
◇ A K
♣ J 7

Dealer: East   **Vulnerability: Both**

S	W	N	E
			3♣
4♠(1)	Pass	5♣(2)	Pass
5◇(2)	Pass	5♡(2)	Pass
6♠	End		

(1) Too good for a simple overcall, South jumps to the spade game in spite of his moderate suit.
(2) Ace-showing cue-bids looking for the spade slam.

Contract: 6♠   **Opening Lead: ♣9**

Declarer won West's nine of clubs lead with dummy's ace in his Six Spade slam, and led a trump to his king, East discarding. His basic plan was to throw the opposition in with a second club, and make them open up hearts. This involved eliminating diamonds first.

On a 2-1 trump split, declarer could have eliminated diamonds completely (ace-king of diamonds, six of trumps to the queen, ruff a diamond, four of trumps to the five, ruff a diamond). The 3-0 trump split robbed declarer of a second trump entry, so he could only partially eliminate diamonds.

Declarer cashed the ace of trumps, then the ace-king of diamonds. He crossed to the queen of trumps, ruffed a third diamond, and then (in the diagrammed ending) exited with a club. Because it was East, crucially with no more diamonds, who was forced to win the second club (as declarer knew from the bidding), the Partial Elimination was wholly successful.

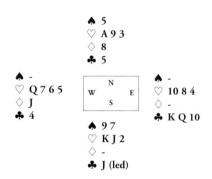

♠ 5
♡ A 9 3
◇ 8
♣ 5

♠ -   N   ♠ -
♡ Q 7 6 5   W   E   ♡ 10 8 4
◇ J   ◇ -
♣ 4   S   ♣ K Q 10

♠ 9 7
♡ K J 2
◇ -
♣ J (led)

East had to broach hearts, because a third club would give ruff-and-discard (a heart from one hand, a ruff in the other). Using the power of dummy's nine, declarer played low from hand, beating West's queen with the ace. His jack was promoted and the slam made.

Note that only queen and ten of hearts offside would beat declarer.

Deal 7

Remember the last deal? This one is similar...but not quite the same.

A different type of Partial Elimination is required for success, and a consideration of East's shape leads to the correct solution.

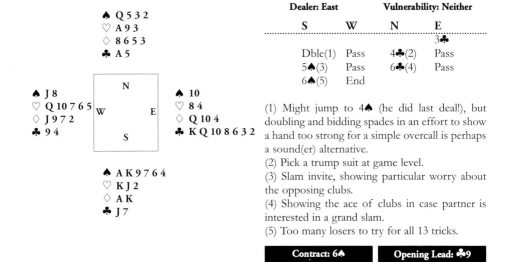

Dealer: East		Vulnerability: Neither	
S	W	N	E
			3♣
Dble(1)	Pass	4♣(2)	Pass
5♠(3)	Pass	6♣(4)	Pass
6♠(5)	End		

(1) Might jump to 4♠ (he did last deal!), but doubling and bidding spades in an effort to show a hand too strong for a simple overcall is perhaps a sound(er) alternative.
(2) Pick a trump suit at game level.
(3) Slam invite, showing particular worry about the opposing clubs.
(4) Showing the ace of clubs in case partner is interested in a grand slam.
(5) Too many losers to try for all 13 tricks.

Contract: 6♠	Opening Lead: ♣9

Declarer won West's nine of clubs lead with the ace, and crossed to the king of trumps, both opponents following. With a Throw-in in mind, declarer immediately set about eliminating diamonds, currently a safe exit for the opposition.

He cashed the ace-king of diamonds, then led the six (note) of trumps to the queen, East discarding (a club). He ruffed a third diamond (with the seven), led the carefully preserved four of trumps over to dummy's five, then ruffed the last diamond. We have reached:

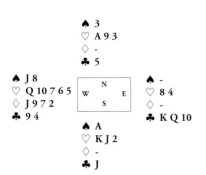

Last deal declarer exited with a club in a similar position (with a diamond in dummy). This time that won't work - a heart return by East will not help with West holding both queen and ten.

This is a solution that is 100%, assuming that East wins the club lead, and holds no more than two hearts. That he will win the club is certain given his bid; that he holds two hearts is also highly likely - after all he advertised seven clubs and has turned up with three diamonds and one trump.

Cash the ace-king of hearts (key plays), stripping East of his hearts, and then exit with the club. East wins, but his forced club return can be trumped in one hand whilst the heart loser is discarded from the other. 12 tricks and slam made.

Deal 8

Is there anything the defence can do to avoid an impending Elimination and Throw-in? The answer, just sometimes, is yes.

Take these positions in which declarer has drawn trumps, holds trumps in both hands, and has eliminated the other suits.

Did declarer play the suit correctly? The answer - assuming he could lead instead from dummy - is no. Play low to his nine, and he endplays West with no winning defence; if East inserts the jack (best - hoping West holds K109), declarer covers with the queen, to force a lead from West around to his nine.

(A)
West	Dummy	East
K10876	A32	J5
	Declarer	
	Q94	

(B)
West	Dummy	East
K10875	A32	Q6
	Declarer	
	J94	

Say declarer can count East for a doubleton. Leading from hand, he crosses to the ace, and East...? If East woodenly plays low, then he will be soon left on play with his jack. On his next lead (of an eliminated suit), declarer will ruff in one hand and throw the third-round loser from the other.

If declarer leads low to dummy's ace, East must jettison his queen, playing for West to hold K10 or better. If East plays low, he will endplayed with his queen.

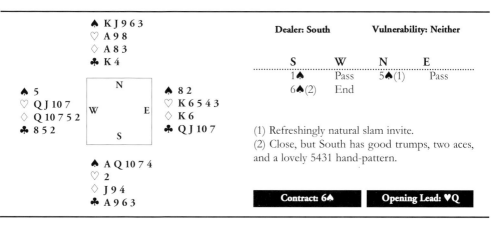

♠ K J 9 6 3
♡ A 9 8
◇ A 8 3
♣ K 4

♠ 5   ♠ 8 2
♡ Q J 10 7   ♡ K 6 5 4 3
◇ Q 10 7 5 2   ◇ K 6
♣ 8 5 2   ♣ Q J 10 7

♠ A Q 10 7 4
♡ 2
◇ J 9 4
♣ A 9 6 3

Dealer: South   **Vulnerability: Neither**

S	W	N	E
1♠	Pass	5♠(1)	Pass
6♠(2)	End		

(1) Refreshingly natural slam invite.
(2) Close, but South has good trumps, two aces, and a lovely 5431 hand-pattern.

Contract: 6♠	**Opening Lead: ♥Q**

Declaring Six Spades, South won the queen of hearts lead with the ace, drew trumps, then eliminated the "rounded suits" (hearts and clubs). He ruffed a heart, crossed to the king of clubs, back to the ace, ruffed a club, ruffed his last heart, and ruffed his last club.

Declarer then cashed the ace of diamonds. East followed low and... I hope not. If East still holds the king of diamonds, he will be left on play with it. His next lead (club/heart) will enable declarer to ruff in one hand and discard a diamond from the other. Slam made.

Provided East jettisons his king of diamonds under the ace (his only chance being that his partner holds Q10), declarer must lose those two tricks: down one.

One final thought. If declarer had cashed that ace of diamonds earlier, would the need to drop his king of diamonds under the ace be so clear to East? I doubt it.

Deal 9

As declarer, say you have drawn trumps, hold extra trumps in both hands, and have eliminated the other suits.

Let us look at some examples of the key suit, the one in which (say) you must throw specifically West in (it has to be West for he cannot profitably lead a second round - into your ace-queen).

(A)	Dummy	
West	432	East
K1086		J75
	Declarer	
	AQ9	

Lead from dummy, planning to insert the nine. West wins cheaply, but has to give ruff-and-discard (you ruff in one hand, and discard a loser from the key suit in the other); or lead into your ace-queen. Perfect.

(B)	Dummy	
West	432	East
K1096		J75
	Declarer	
	AQ8	

Similarly, you lead from dummy to your eight, endplaying West.

My question is as follows: is there anything the defence can do? The answer is maybe. East must insert the jack.

In (A) this is a valiant effort to no effect, as declarer can cover with the queen, using his remaining A9 to act like AQ (preventing the return of the suit from West). In (B), however, East's jack will prevent the endplay. Declarer covers with the queen, and West's "spots" are good enough. He wins the king and fires back the ten, thus promoting his nine.

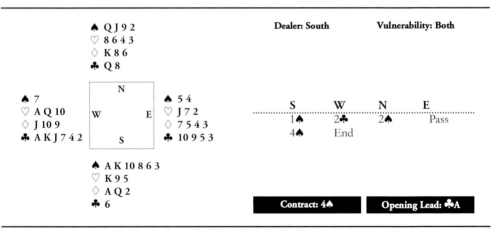

	♠ Q J 9 2		**Dealer: South**		**Vulnerability: Both**
	♡ 8 6 4 3				
	◇ K 8 6				
	♣ Q 8				

	S	**W**	**N**	**E**
	1♠	2♣	2♠	Pass
	4♠	End		

West: ♠ 7 · ♡ A Q 10 · ◇ J 10 9 · ♣ A K J 7 4 2

East: ♠ 5 4 · ♡ J 7 2 · ◇ 7 5 4 3 · ♣ 10 9 5 3

South: ♠ A K 10 8 6 3 · ♡ K 9 5 · ◇ A Q 2 · ♣ 6

Contract: 4♠ **Opening Lead: ♣A**

Our featured deal sees just such a second-hand-high play break up an intended Throw-in. West led out the ace-king of clubs, declarer ruffing the second. Trumps were drawn and diamonds cashed, finishing with dummy's king.

At Trick Eight declarer led a heart from dummy, and it was East's big moment. If he played low, declarer would insert the nine. West would win the ten but be forced to lead away from his ace-queen, or lead a club, allowing declarer to ruff in dummy and discard a heart from hand, thereby restricting his heart losers to two.

East made no mistake, however, inserting the jack of hearts (key play). If declarer ducked, West could underplay with the ten, and if declarer covered with the king, West could win his ace then the queen-ten. Down one.

Question: Can you make if West switches to a diamond at Trick Two? Answer next deal.

Deal 10

At the end of the last deal (Deal 9) I posed a question (look back).

You cannot make Four Spades if West begins with two top clubs, even if you ruff, draw trumps, eliminate diamonds, and lead a heart from dummy. For East prevents the impending Throw-in on West by inserting the jack.

If West cashes one top club and switches to the jack of diamonds at Trick Two, however, you can win. Draw trumps, and eliminate diamonds finishing in dummy (as before). This time you still have the queen of clubs. Lead it and - key play - discard a heart from hand. This Loser-on-Loser play endplays West into leading a third club and giving a ruff-and-discard (ruff in dummy, throw a heart from hand); or leading a heart from the ace. Game made.

Elimination and Throw-in - what to look out for:

(A) *Declarer*

Look out for... Plenty of trumps, suits that can be eliminated, and a suit you would rather an opponent lead. You'll then need an exit card.

(B) *Defence*

Look out for... Getting rid of short honours (to prevent you being endplayed); second-hand high (to prevent partner being endplayed).

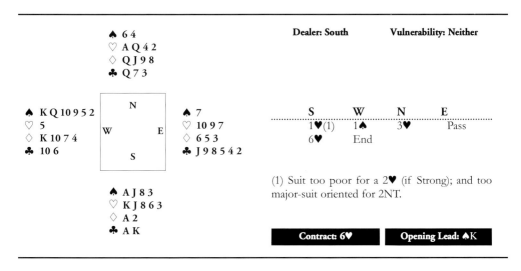

	♠ 6 4	
	♡ A Q 4 2	
	◇ Q J 9 8	
	♣ Q 7 3	

♠ K Q 10 9 5 2		♠ 7
♡ 5		♡ 10 9 7
◇ K 10 7 4		◇ 6 5 3
♣ 10 6		♣ J 9 8 5 4 2

	♠ A J 8 3	
	♡ K J 8 6 3	
	◇ A 2	
	♣ A K	

Dealer: South   **Vulnerability: Neither**

S	W	N	E
1♥(1)	1♠	3♥	Pass
6♥	End		

(1) Suit too poor for a 2♥ (if Strong); and too major-suit oriented for 2NT.

| **Contract: 6♥** | **Opening Lead:** ♠K |

This Elimination and Throw-in comes from over 50 years ago, and features a very young Eddie Kantar, that most brilliant of teachers from across the pond. Winning the king of spades lead, declarer found a line to succeed with the king of diamonds offside and trumps 3-1. He cashed two top trumps, then the ace-king of clubs and the ace of diamonds. A third trump over to dummy drew East's last trump, the queen of clubs was cashed, discarding the diamond, then a spade led to the eight.

West won the nine, but was endplayed. Another spade would promote declarer's jack; and a diamond would create a trick for dummy's honours. Slam made.

Deal 11

One critical ingredient for an Elimination and Throw-in is trumps in both hands. This is so that the ruff-and-discard return gains you a trick.

Contrast the following two-card endings, with spades as trumps and West, thrown in, on lead:

(A)

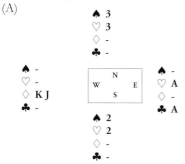

The forced diamond lead gains you a trick in (A). You ruff in one hand, and discard the heart loser from the other, whereupon you can ruff the heart (the key difference).

(B)

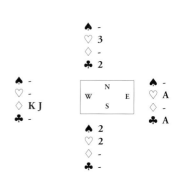

In (B) you can discard dummy's heart and ruff in hand, but this does you no good as you cannot then ruff your heart in dummy. The Throw-in has gained nothing.

However there are Throw-ins of a different nature that gain tricks without having trumps in both hands. Take our featured Notrump contract.

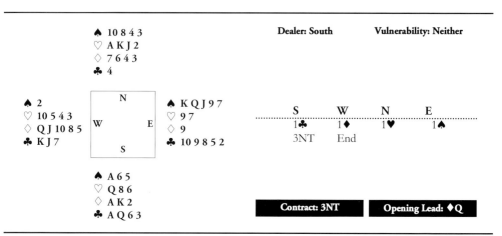

		Dealer: South		Vulnerability: Neither

♠ 10 8 4 3
♡ A K J 2
◇ 7 6 4 3
♣ 4

♠ 2 — ♠ K Q J 9 7
♡ 10 5 4 3 — ♡ 9 7
◇ Q J 10 8 5 — ◇ 9
♣ K J 7 — ♣ 10 9 8 5 2

♠ A 6 5
♡ Q 8 6
◇ A K 2
♣ A Q 6 3

S	W	N	E
1♣	1◆	1♥	1♠
3NT	End		

Contract: 3NT **Opening Lead: ◆Q**

A revealing auction tells you that West holds five diamonds, and East five spades (overcallers do not - should not - introduce four-card suits). Win West's diamond lead with the king, and cash your five major-suit winners, stripping West of all his cards in those suits.

Now play the ace of diamonds and exit with a diamond. West is welcome to take his three remaining winners, for you know what his next play must be: a club (for that is all he can have left). This ensures that your queen of the suit is promoted - your ninth trick.

Such Throw-ins without trumps in both hands often involve pressurising the opponent into making fatal discards - the Strip Squeeze. More on this later.

Deal 12

Of the three basic types of endplay (the Throw-in, the Trump Coup and the Squeeze), we move from the Throw-in to the Trump Coup.

Take a trump holding of:

West   Dummy   East
   ♠A2
♠6   ♠J987
   Declarer
   ♠KQ10543

You cash the ace and lead to your queen, naturally hoping for a 3-2 split. When West discards, it appears that you have a certain loser, because you have no trump left in dummy with which to lead, in order to finesse against East's guarded jack. Is all lost?

No. You need to reach the following ending:

   Dummy
West   Anything   East
Anything   ♠J9
   Declarer
   ♠K10

If the lead is in your hand, you are are sunk, forced to cash the king and give East the last trick. But if the lead is in dummy (crucially), then you must make the last two tricks. Dummy's card (which is totally irrelevant) sees East perforce trump, enabling you to overtrump cheaply.

Note the importance of having the same trump length as East; hold a third trump in hand (in a three-card ending with the lead in dummy), and you would be forced to ruff dummy's card, then lead away from your own hand. No good. One crucial component of bringing about a Trump Coup is therefore reducing your trump length.

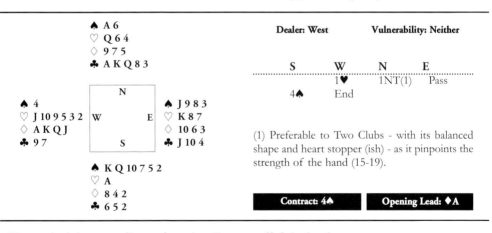

Dealer: West   **Vulnerability: Neither**

S	W	N	E
	1♥	1NT(1)	Pass
4♠	End		

(1) Preferable to Two Clubs - with its balanced shape and heart stopper (ish) - as it pinpoints the strength of the hand (15-19).

Contract: 4♠	**Opening Lead: ♦A**

West cashed three top diamonds against Four Spades, then switched to the jack of hearts. Winning his ace, declarer crossed to the ace of trumps, and returned to his queen, West discarding.

Declarer needed to reduce his trumps down to the same length as East. He therefore crossed to the queen of clubs and ruffed a heart; he crossed to the king of clubs and ruffed the last heart.

With two remaining trumps - same as East - declarer crossed to the ace of clubs (needing East to follow a third time), and now had the perfect Trump Coup. He led anything from dummy (actually a club), and overruffed East's nine of trumps with the ten, scoring the last trick with his king (beating East's jack). 10 tricks and game made.

Deal 13

To further our understanding of the Trump Coup, let us remind ourselves of the previous deal:

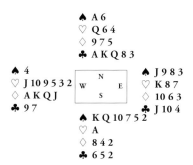

```
            ♠ A 6
            ♡ Q 6 4
            ◇ 9 7 5
            ♣ A K Q 8 3
♠ 4                          ♠ J 9 8 3
♡ J 10 9 5 3 2    N          ♡ K 8 7
◇ A K Q J      W     E       ◇ 10 6 3
♣ 9 7             S          ♣ J 10 4
            ♠ K Q 10 7 5 2
            ♡ A
            ◇ 8 4 2
            ♣ 6 5 2
```

Declaring Four Spades after West leads three top diamonds and switches to the jack of hearts, you win the ace, cross to the ace of trumps, return to your king (West discarding), then need to pick up East's jack of trumps without a trump in dummy. You must:

(1) Reduce your trump length to the same as East's by ruffing.

(2) Finish in dummy at Trick 11.

This you can do by crossing twice to a club and ruffing a heart, then crossing to a third club (East following - phew!) in order to lead through East's ♠J9 to your remaining ♠K10. Game made.

You needed three dummy entries to pull off (1) and (2) above; two to ruff down to the same number of trumps, and one to return to dummy for the Trick 12 lead. You have three dummy entries in clubs, but *what would have happened if West had switched to a club (not a heart) at Trick Four?*

You would have needed to use the ace of trumps as a dummy entry, and therefore would need to anticipate the bad split before it came to light. The correct line is: win the club, cross to the queen of trumps, cash the ace of hearts, return to the ace of trumps (West discarding), ruff a heart, cross to a club, ruff a heart, then cross to a third club for the Trick 12 Coup.

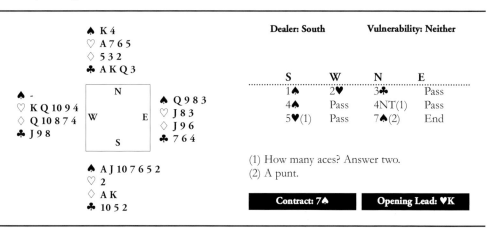

```
            ♠ K 4
            ♡ A 7 6 5
            ◇ 5 3 2
            ♣ A K Q 3
♠ -                          ♠ Q 9 8 3
♡ K Q 10 9 4     N           ♡ J 8 3
◇ Q 10 8 7 4  W     E        ◇ J 9 6
♣ J 9 8          S           ♣ 7 6 4
            ♠ A J 10 7 6 5 2
            ♡ 2
            ◇ A K
            ♣ 10 5 2
```

Dealer: South   Vulnerability: Neither

S	W	N	E
1♠	2♥	3♣	Pass
4♠	Pass	4NT(1)	Pass
5♥(1)	Pass	7♠(2)	End

(1) How many aces? Answer two.
(2) A punt.

Contract: 7♠   **Opening Lead: ♥K**

On this grand slam deal, West leads the king of hearts to your ace. If you cash the king of trumps at Trick Two, you have gone down. You must anticipate a bad split and, at no cost, ruff a heart at Trick Two (key play). Now a trump to the king, trump to the ten, ace-king of diamonds, club to the queen, ruff a heart, club to the king, ruff a heart, club to the ace, and you're home.

By dint of the heart ruff at Trick Two, you have reduced down to two trumps - as East - and the lead is in dummy. The lead of either card sees you overruff East's ♠Q9 with your ♠AJ. 13 tricks and grand slam made.

Deal 14

In common parlance, a "Coup" is (I quote) "a brilliant and successful stroke or action". In Bridge it has a more specific meaning: without further designation, it refers to an endplay situation in which a defender's finesseable trumps are trapped without a finesse.

To bring about such a Coup, you must:
(1) Reduce your trump length to the same as the opponent's by ruffing.
(2) Finish in dummy, typically at Trick 11.

Sometimes, seemingly drastic measures are called for, such as trumping dummy's winners. This is then known as a Grand Coup - take this ending with hearts trumps, and the lead in dummy (See across):

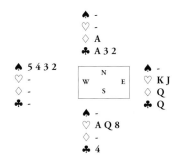

You need to reduce your trumps down to East's doubleton, so must ruff dummy's ace of diamonds (you are all winners outside trumps so this should be no hardship). Now cross to the ace of clubs, and you have reached the classic Coup position. With the lead in dummy, you can overruff East's ♥KJ cheaply to avoid a loser.

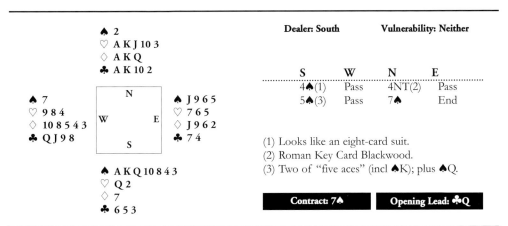

Dealer: South		Vulnerability: Neither	
S	W	N	E
4♠(1)	Pass	4NT(2)	Pass
5♠(3)	Pass	7♠	End

(1) Looks like an eight-card suit.
(2) Roman Key Card Blackwood.
(3) Two of "five aces" (incl ♠K); plus ♠Q.

Contract: 7♠	Opening Lead: ♣Q

This deal required Grand Coup technique: no fewer than three of dummy's winners needed to be ruffed in order to achieve success (a "Triple Grand Coup").

Win West's queen of clubs lead (unfortunate - but at least it wasn't a trump), and cross to the ace-king of trumps. West discarding is a blow, and now you need a Coup, entailing ruffing three times in your hand then using a fourth dummy entry to finish there at Trick 11. The only way home is to...

Cross to a diamond and ruff a winning diamond; cross to a heart and ruff another winning diamond; cross to a heart and ruff a winning heart; now finesse the ten of clubs (marked by West's lead) and lead another winning heart.

If East ruffs, overruff cheaply, draw his trump, and score the last trick with a top club in dummy. If East discards, throw your club and "coup" him with ♠Q10 over ♠J9. 13 tricks and grand slam made.

Deal 15

This is the classic Trump Coup, with spades as trumps:

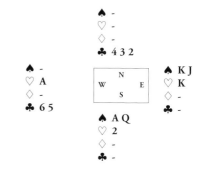

	Dummy	
West	Anything	East
Anything		♠J9
	Declarer	
	♠K10	

Although we have so far focussed on the need to lead from dummy at Trick 12, you will score these last two tricks if any player apart from yourself is leading.

If there is no way to reach dummy, you can make the last two tricks in the following ending (spades trumps, lead in your hand) by exiting with your losing heart:

You do not mind which opponent wins the heart; with East holding the king of trumps, you are bound to score your both your trumps.

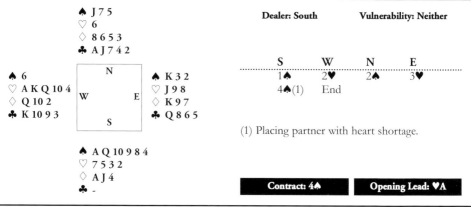

Dealer: South		Vulnerability: Neither	
S	W	N	E
1♠	2♥	2♠	3♥
4♠(1)	End		

(1) Placing partner with heart shortage.

Contract: 4♠	Opening Lead: ♥A

On this deal, you as declarer can make Four Spades with six fewer points than the opponents. West leads the the ace of hearts, and hurriedly switches to his singleton trump in an effort to cut down heart ruffs in dummy. You try dummy's jack, in the hope of tempting a cover, but East wisely withholds his king, a sure sign that he has three cards.

Needing to use both dummy's remaining trumps to ruff hearts, you cash the ace of clubs discarding (say) a diamond. You then ruff a club, cash the ace of diamonds (before anybody throws all their diamonds away), ruff a heart, ruff a club, ruff a heart, and ruff a club. This is the four-card ending:

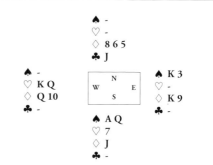

Exit with either red card, and you must come to your ♠AQ. 10 tricks and game made. Note the key trump-shortening technique that was necessary to score all your six trumps in hand.

Deal 16

In our look at Trump Endings, study the following position, with hearts as trumps.

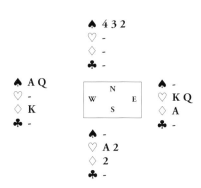

It looks as though you can win just one trick, your ace of trumps. And that is indeed so, if you (S) are on lead. But what if dummy (N) leads?

Even though dummy is leading a loser (spade), you cannot be prevented from making your two of trumps "en passant". For if East discards, you simply ruff with the two; and if East ruffs in, away goes your losing diamond, and you then score the last two tricks. [Note that you could equally well reduce the above position to a two-card ending (removing the ace and king of trumps), and a lead from dummy would similarly promote the two.]

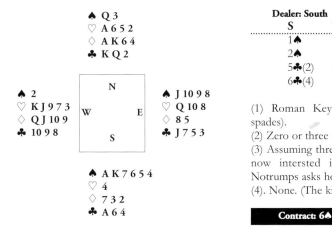

Dealer: South		Vulnerability: Neither	
S	**W**	**N**	**E**
1♠	Pass	2♦	Pass
2♠	Pass	4NT(1)	Pass
5♣(2)	Pass	5NT(3)	Pass
6♣(4)	Pass	6♠	End

(1) Roman Key Card Blackwood (agreeing spades).
(2) Zero or three of "five aces" (including ♠K).
(3) Assuming three key cards opposite, North is now intersted in a grand slam. His Five Notrumps asks how many kings partner holds.
(4). None. (The king of trumps is an "ace").

Contract: 6♠	Opening Lead: ♦Q

Witness this slam deal. Winning West's diamond lead with dummy's king, you cash the queen of spades and cross to the king. West discarding is a real blow, for it appears you have an unavoidable diamond loser in addition to your trump. Not so - think in terms of winning 12 tricks rather than avoiding losing two, and you can prevail.

Cash the ace of trumps (optional), then play to make your low trumps en passant. Cross to the ace of hearts and ruff a heart; cash the three clubs (before East can throw them away) finishing in dummy, and ruff a third heart.

Now cross to the ace of diamonds and, in a two-card ending in which East holds a club and the master trump, and you hold a losing diamond and a smaller trump, lead the fourth heart.

If East discards, you ruff; if East ruffs, you discard the diamond, and score your trump at Trick 13. 12 tricks and slam made.

Deal 17

We are learning to how "elope" with our small trumps (spades in each example below).

In the first diagram, you can score your small trump "en passant" provided dummy (or West) leads:

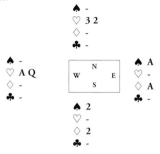

If East discards, you ruff; if East ruffs, you discard. Infuriating for East, who would claim the last two tricks if he was on lead.

Note that the ending works because you are playing *after* East. Swap the defensive hands around, and you could not win a trick. Alter their cards slightly, though, and you can score your small trump even when the bigger trump is on your left. Take this diagram (spades trumps):

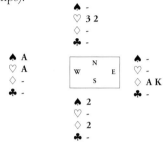

You can score a trick here, but only if dummy is on lead. You ruff a heart and, because West has to follow suit, the trick is yours.

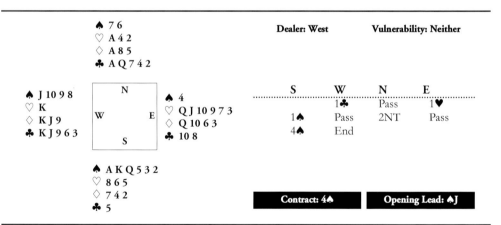

S	W	N	E
	1♣	Pass	1♡
1♠	Pass	2NT	Pass
4♠	End		

Dealer: West   Vulnerability: Neither

Contract: 4♠   **Opening Lead: ♠J**

On this Four Spade deal, West led a trump (for the lack of an attractive alternative). Declarer won and cashed two more top trumps, disappointed to see the split. He seemed booked for more than three losers, but watch him garner ten winners.

At Trick Four declarer finessed the queen of clubs (marked on the bidding). He cashed the ace, discarding a red card, ruffed a third club, crossed to a red ace, ruffed a fourth club with his penultimate trump, crossed to the other red ace, and ruffed the last club with his last trump.

10 tricks and game made leaving both opponents holding three winners. West's opening lead was perfectly reasonable, but a red-suit would have removed a dummy entry prematurely, and rendered the game unmakeable.

There are other fascinating and complex endings revolving around trumps which we will revisit later in the book. Next deal we will begin to tackle the Squeeze.

Deal 18

A Squeeze is a play which forces an opponent, with an embarrass de riches, to discard at a time when he would prefer not to. The term was coined by US great Sidney Lenz back in the 1920s.

It is a generally held belief that Squeeze-play is the domain of the expert. But this need not be so, as many Squeezes simply play themselves. Witness this deal, in which all declarer needs to do is keep his head and watch out for one card.

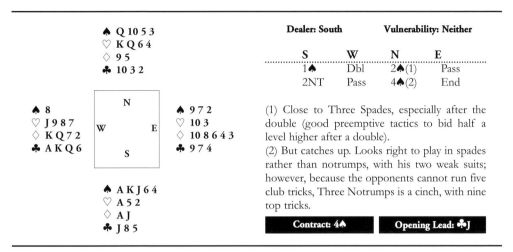

	♠ Q 10 5 3	
	♡ K Q 6 4	
	◇ 9 5	
	♣ 10 3 2	

♠ 8		♠ 9 7 2
♡ J 9 8 7		♡ 10 3
◇ K Q 7 2		◇ 10 8 6 4 3
♣ A K Q 6		♣ 9 7 4

	♠ A K J 6 4	
	♡ A 5 2	
	◇ A J	
	♣ J 8 5	

Dealer: South **Vulnerability: Neither**

S	W	N	E
1♠	Dbl	2♠(1)	Pass
2NT	Pass	4♠(2)	End

(1) Close to Three Spades, especially after the double (good preemptive tactics to bid half a level higher after a double).

(2) But catches up. Looks right to play in spades rather than notrumps, with his two weak suits; however, because the opponents cannot run five club tricks, Three Notrumps is a cinch, with nine top tricks.

| **Contract: 4♠** | **Opening Lead: ♣J** |

West naturally cashes three top clubs, then switches to the king of diamonds. Ostensibly, it looks as though you as declarer need a 3-3 heart split for your tenth trick. Actually you are far better placed, especially given that West has advertised the queen of diamonds and is likely to have four hearts for his double of One Spade.

Play out all your trumps - yes - don't stop playing trumps because your opponents have run out. As you play the last trump, West will find it impossible to discard. Here is the ending:

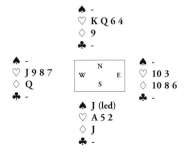

	♠ -	
	♡ K Q 6 4	
	◇ 9	
	♣ -	

♠ -		♠ -
♡ J 9 8 7		♡ 10 3
◇ Q		◇ 10 8 6
♣ -		♣ -

	♠ J (led)	
	♡ A 5 2	
	◇ J	
	♣ -	

If West lets go of a heart, dummy's hearts will provide four tricks. West can see that, so in practice will discard the queen of diamonds, hoping his partner can guard the suit with the jack.

No good. The queen of diamonds was the one card you were looking out for. If you did not see it, you would play out dummy's hearts in the hope of a fourth-round length winner. But with West's queen of diamonds going, you can table the jack, a promoted winner. 10 tricks and game made.

You pulled off a Simple Automatic Squeeze: Simple, because just one opponent was squeezed; Automatic, because the Squeeze would have worked on either opponent, provided they alone guarded both red suits.

Deal 19

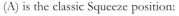

(A) is the classic Squeeze position:

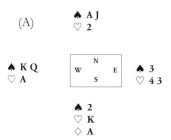

South leads the ace of diamonds and West, because he alone guards both spades and hearts, has no good discard. Throw a spade and dummy's jack is promoted; throw a heart and declarer's king is promoted.

(B)

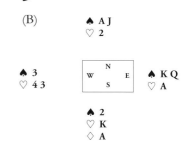

In (B) (swapping the defenders hands) East is identically squeezed on the ace of diamonds (dummy's heart going). Because either opponent, provided they uniquely guard each major-suit, is squeezed, the position is "Automatic".

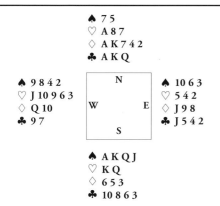

Dealer: South **Vulnerability: Neither**

S	W	N	E
1♠	Pass	2♦	Pass
2NT	Pass	7NT(1)	End

(1) Even with 20 fabulous-looking points, this is a stretch facing partner's 15-16. 37 is the high-card-point guide for 7NT.

Contract: 7NT	**Opening Lead: ♥J**

On our featured grand slam deal, declarer counted 12 top tricks. His non-Squeeze chance of a thirteenth was the jack of clubs falling in three rounds, promoting the ten.

Winning the heart lead, declarer unblocked the other top heart, then led over to the three top clubs. No jack fell, West discarding a heart, so a Squeeze was his only chance. He needed the opponent who held the jack of clubs to hold at least three diamonds (making him the sole guarder of the suit).

Declarer cashed the ace of hearts, discarding a diamond, then ran his spades. This was the position as the last spade was led:

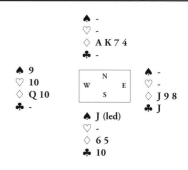

What could East discard? A diamond would give dummy the last three tricks, and the jack of clubs would promote declarer's ten. 13 tricks and grand slam made. Note the same fate would have befallen West should he have held East's cards (an Automatic Squeeze).

Deal 20

In (A) below, West is squeezed on the ace of hearts lead, holding sole guard of both diamonds and clubs. If East held West's cards, he too would de squeezed (an Automatic Squeeze).

West is squeezed on the ace of hearts, as he has to discard before North. Swap the East-West cards, however...

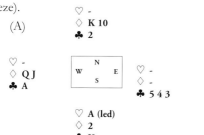

(A)

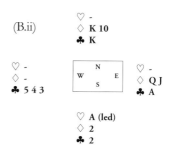

(B.ii)

Let us now move the king of clubs to North, and compare.

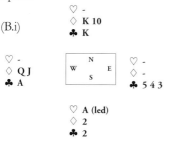

(B.i)

...and East is not squeezed.

By moving the king of clubs, North's hand now contains both the two-card guard (♦K10) and the one-card guard (♣K). Because North has to discard before East, the squeeze does not operate. This is a "Positional Squeeze" because only one defender (here West, discarding first) can be squeezed.

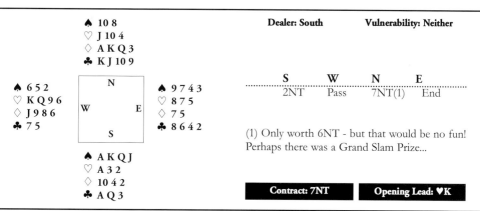

	♠ 10 8	
	♡ J 10 4	
	◇ A K Q 3	
	♣ K J 10 9	
♠ 6 5 2	N	♠ 9 7 4 3
♡ K Q 9 6		♡ 8 7 5
◇ J 9 8 6	W E	◇ 7 5
♣ 7 5	S	♣ 8 6 4 2
	♠ A K Q J	
	♡ A 3 2	
	◇ 10 4 2	
	♣ A Q 3	

Dealer: South   Vulnerability: Neither

S	W	N	E
2NT	Pass	7NT(1)	End

(1) Only worth 6NT - but that would be no fun! Perhaps there was a Grand Slam Prize...

Contract: 7NT   Opening Lead: ♥K

Declarer won West's king of hearts lead, cashed the ace-king of diamonds (in case the jack fell), then the clubs, and then the spades. As the last spade was led, West had to discard - fatally - between ♥Q and ♦J9. Whichever suit he released, dummy (holding ♥J and ♦Q3) would keep. 13 tricks and grand slam made.

Note, however, that if the East-West hands were swapped, East would escape. No Squeeze would operate, because dummy, holding both the guards (♥J and ♦Q3), would have to discard before East. East could follow his discard, and score the last trick. It was, therefore, a Positional Squeeze.

Deal 21

A typical Squeeze involves two suits. If the same opponent uniquely guards both, there is potential for a Squeeze.

Say the declaring side has a two-card "threat", ♠AJ; a defender holding ♠KQ needs to retain both cards. Note that ♠AJ may be termed a "Weak Threat" because both opponents may be guarding it (if ♠K and ♠Q are in different hands).

Say the declaring side also has a one-card threat (say ♥K). This is a "Strong Threat", because only one defender (the one with ♥A) can guard it. If the same defender holds both ♠KQ and ♥A, he is in trouble. Declarer needs to play out all his winners and, crucially, be in the other hand to the two-card threat (♠AJ).

Let us consider some positions, and see whether a Squeeze operates on the ace of diamonds lead:

(A) is a non-starter. West guards spades and East hearts. No squeeze can possibly operate (unless there is a third suit - more anon). In (B) and (C), the two-card threat (♠AJ) is in North, the one-card threat (♥K) in South. As an Automatic Squeeze, both West (in B) and East (in C) are squeezed. In (D) and (E), both threats are in North, rendering the Squeeze Positional.

It succeeds if the defensive guards are discarding before (i.e. West is squeezed in D); but not so after (East escapes in E).

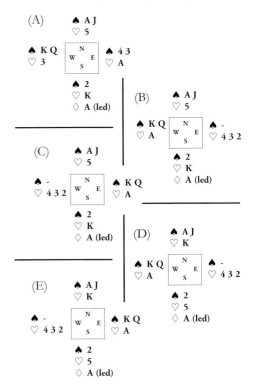

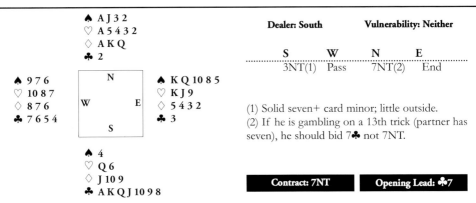

Dealer: South   Vulnerability: Neither

S	W	N	E
3NT(1)	Pass	7NT(2)	End

(1) Solid seven+ card minor; little outside.
(2) If he is gambling on a 13th trick (partner has seven), he should bid 7♣ not 7NT.

Contract: 7NT	Opening Lead: ♣7

Declarer won the club lead in hand, and ran all his clubs, cleverly discarding all dummy's diamonds. He then cashed his diamonds, hoping for a major-suit Squeeze. But because dummy held both threats, and East was discarding afterwards, no Squeeze operated - analogous to (E). Down one.

Deal 22

Let us revisit the previous deal. Declaring Seven Notrumps (don't ask), South received a club lead. He ran his clubs, discarding dummy's diamonds, then cashed his diamonds. But because East was discarding after dummy (with its threats in both majors), no Squeeze operated. Down one.

There was no way for declarer to succeed on a club lead, but say West led a diamond. Declarer can now make all 13 tricks by converting the ending from a Positional Squeeze to an Automatic one.

He does this by cashing the ace of hearts (key play) prior to running his clubs. [He cannot do this on a club lead, for the lack of a re-entry to hand.] This moves the one-card threat to South. With the two-card threat (♠AJ) in the other hand to the one-card threat (♥Q), the Squeeze is now Automatic.

Effectively an unblocking play, this ingeniously simple manoeuvre of cashing a winner to move a threat to the other hand, thereby converting a Positional Squeeze into an Automatic one, is known as a Vienna Coup (a name originating from Whist; the Austrian connection has been lost in the midst of time).

Here is the ending as declarer leads the final club:

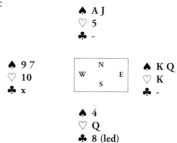

The heart is thrown from dummy, and East surrenders.

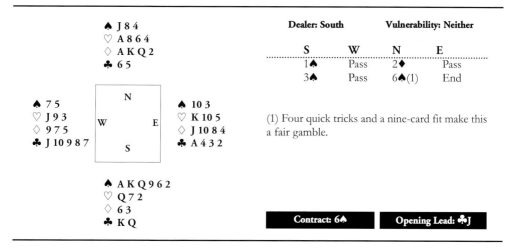

The defence play ace and another club against Six Spades. Declarer wins, draws trumps in two rounds, then makes the key play of cashing the ace of hearts (the Vienna Coup). Only by doing this is he later able to squeeze East.

Declarer now runs all his trumps, leaving ♥Q in hand and ♦AKQ2 in dummy. What can East throw (on the last trump) from ♥K and ♦J1084? Answer: the towel!

Deal 23

Contrast the following Squeeze-endings:

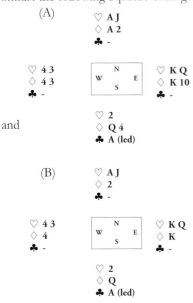

(A)

♡ A J
◇ A 2
♣ -

♡ 4 3   ♡ K Q
◇ 4 3   ◇ K 10
♣ -   ♣ -

and

♡ 2
◇ Q 4
♣ A (led)

(B)

♡ A J
◇ 2
♣ -

♡ 4 3   ♡ K Q
◇ 4   ◇ K
♣ -   ♣ -

♡ 2
◇ Q
♣ A (led)

In (A), no Squeeze (on East) operates. For you have no good discard from dummy on your ace of clubs. Whichever red-suit you throw, East does the same and scores the last trick.

In (B), however, East is squeezed. You throw dummy's diamond on the ace of clubs and East has no good discard.

To convert (A) into (B), you needed to have cashed dummy's ace of diamonds earlier, thus converting a Positional Squeeze (one that would only work on West, were he to hold East's cards) into an Automatic one (successful against either player). Cashing the ace of diamonds is known as a Vienna Coup. Here's another...

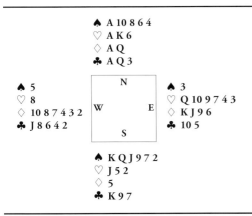

♠ A 10 8 6 4
♡ A K 6
◇ A Q
♣ A Q 3

♠ 5   ♠ 3
♡ 8   ♡ Q 10 9 7 4 3
◇ 10 8 7 4 3 2   ◇ K J 9 6
♣ J 8 6 4 2   ♣ 10 5

♠ K Q J 9 7 2
♡ J 5 2
◇ 5
♣ K 9 7

Dealer: East   **Vulnerability: Both**

S	W	N	E
			2♥(1)
2♠	Pass	7♠(2)	Pass

(1) Weak Two - 5-10 points and a good six-card suit.
(2) Should settle for Six because of his lack of a side-suit or a singleton.

Contract: 7♠   **Opening Lead: ♥8**

You reach the dizzy heights of Seven Spades on West's heart lead. The bidding has told you that East has the guarded queen of hearts and also, in all probability, the king of diamonds (how else could he muster up a vulnerable bid, albeit a mini-preempt?).

Don't despair that the diamond finesse looks doomed. Win the heart, draw trumps, then, crucially, cash dummy's other top heart (the Vienna Coup), Now that the one-card heart threat is in your hand (♥J), and the two-card diamond threat (♦AQ) is in dummy, you can squeeze East by simply cashing your winners, (something you could not have done without releasing the other top heart).

On the last black-suit winner (dummy retaining ♦AQ), East must discard from ♥Q and ♦KJ. Throw the heart and your jack is promoted; throw the diamond and a diamond to the ace fells the king. 13 tricks and grand slam made.

Deal 24

The Squeeze is all about pressure; playing the last trump; giving the hapless opponent an impossible discard. Bearing that in mind, contrast the following endings:

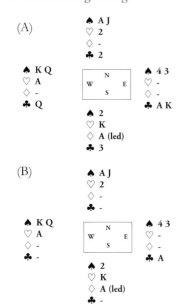

(A)

```
              ♠ A J
              ♡ 2
              ◇ -
              ♣ 2
♠ K Q                      ♠ 4 3
♡ A          N             ♡ -
◇ -        W   E           ◇ -
♣ Q          S             ♣ A K
              ♠ 2
              ♡ K
              ◇ A (led)
              ♣ 3
```

(B)

```
              ♠ A J
              ♡ 2
              ◇ -
              ♣ -
♠ K Q                      ♠ 4 3
♡ A          N             ♡ -
◇ -        W   E           ◇ -
♣ -          S             ♣ A
              ♠ 2
              ♡ K
              ◇ A (led)
              ♣ -
```

Although it looks bad for West in (A), in fact he will survive. For he has an "idle card", the queen of clubs, which he can painlessly discard on the ace of diamonds. He retains both his major-suit guards, and there is no extra trick. Not so in (B), a classic Squeeze position, in which West has no answer on the ace of diamonds.

Question: What did you need to do to convert (A) into (B)?

Answer: you needed to lose a club earlier.

For a Squeeze to operate, you need to have *one fewer winner than the number of cards remaining* (sometimes referred to as "N-1"). In (B) you had two winners and three-cards remaining - perfect; in (A) you had two winners and four cards - no good. In order to reach a position whereby you have one fewer winner than the number of tricks left, you may need to *"Rectify the Count"* (lose a trick).

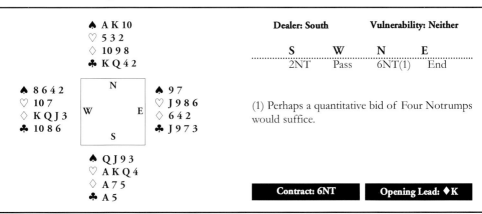

```
              ♠ A K 10
              ♡ 5 3 2
              ◇ 10 9 8
              ♣ K Q 4 2
♠ 8 6 4 2       N          ♠ 9 7
♡ 10 7                     ♡ J 9 8 6
◇ K Q J 3   W      E       ◇ 6 4 2
♣ 10 8 6                   ♣ J 9 7 3
                S
              ♠ Q J 9 3
              ♡ A K Q 4
              ◇ A 7 5
              ♣ A 5
```

Dealer: South   **Vulnerability: Neither**

S	W	N	E
2NT	Pass	6NT(1)	End

(1) Perhaps a quantitative bid of Four Notrumps would suffice.

Contract: 6NT	**Opening Lead: ◆K**

Declaring Six Notrumps on our featured deal, South counted 11 top tricks on West's king of diamonds lead. A 3-3 heart split would give him his slam, but South sought better.

With 11 winners and all 13 tricks remaining, declarer needed to rectify the count to reach "N-1". He therefore ducked the opening lead (key play).

Winning the queen of diamonds at Trick Two, declarer cashed his four top spades. On the third, East could spade his last diamond, but on the fourth? If declarer had won the first trick, East would have another "idle" diamond, but as it was, he had to discard a heart or a club. Both fatally. 12 tricks and slam made.

Deal 25

A normal Squeeze will only operate is there is precisely one fewer winner than the number of cards left ("N-1").

So when you have identified the need for a Squeeze, make sure you have all the remaining tricks bar one. To reach this state, you may need to lose trick(s), a process known as "*rectifying the count*".

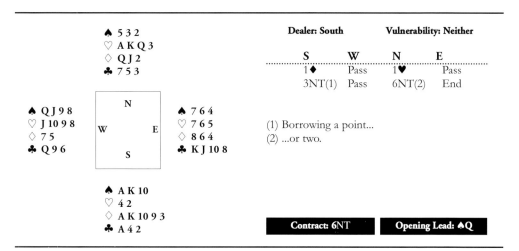

♠ 5 3 2			
♡ A K Q 3			
◇ Q J 2			
♣ 7 5 3			

Dealer: South   **Vulnerability: Neither**

S	W	N	E
1♦	Pass	1♥	Pass
3NT(1)	Pass	6NT(2)	End

(1) Borrowing a point...
(2) ...or two.

♠ Q J 9 8		♠ 7 6 4
♡ J 10 9 8		♡ 7 6 5
◇ 7 5		◇ 8 6 4
♣ Q 9 6		♣ K J 10 8

♠ A K 10
♡ 4 2
◇ A K 10 9 3
♣ A 4 2

Contract: 6NT   **Opening Lead: ♠Q**

Overbidding to Six Notrumps on our featured deal, you count up 11 top tricks. You envisage a Squeeze-ending, partly because there is no other hope of a twelfth trick, and more especially because there are two suits (spades and hearts) that need guarding, and only one opponent can guard each (they are both Strong Threats; only one opponent can hold at least four hearts). The opening lead has told you that West guards spades; you must hope he also guards hearts.

The problem is that you have 11 winners, and there are still 13 tricks to play. To reach the correct ending (and a good tip is to try to visualise this in your mind), you need to rectify the count*, in other words to lose an early trick. *You can actually succeed without rectifying the count (if you read the ending) using Strip Squeeze technique - more anon.

The correct line is to win the queen of spades lead and, at Trick Two, duck a club (key play). Say East wins and returns a spade. You win, and now run all your minor-suit winners. As you cash the last diamond, West will have to discard in the five-card ending (see across), a discard he will not enjoy:

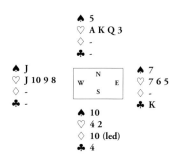

	♠ 5	
	♡ A K Q 3	
	◇ -	
	♣ -	

♠ J		♠ 7
♡ J 10 9 8		♡ 7 6 5
◇ -		◇ -
♣ -		♣ K

♠ 10
♡ 4 2
◇ 10 (led)
♣ 4

If West discards a heart, dummy's hearts will all be good. In practice West is likely to let go a spade, in the hope that his partner can guard the suit with the ten. No good this time. You cash the promoted ten of spades, and take the last three tricks with dummy's top hearts. 12 tricks and slam made.

Deal 26

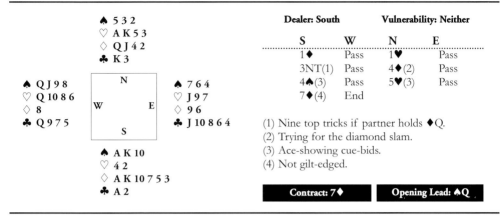

	♠ 5 3 2		
	♡ A K 5 3		
	◇ Q J 4 2		
	♣ K 3		

♠ Q J 9 8		♠ 7 6 4
♡ Q 10 8 6	N	♡ J 9 7
◇ 8	W E	◇ 9 6
♣ Q 9 7 5	S	♣ J 10 8 6 4

	♠ A K 10
	♡ 4 2
	◇ A K 10 7 5 3
	♣ A 2

S	W	N	E
1◇	Pass	1♥	Pass
3NT(1)	Pass	4◇(2)	Pass
4♠(3)	Pass	5♥(3)	Pass
7◇(4)	End		

(1) Nine top tricks if partner holds ◆Q.
(2) Trying for the diamond slam.
(3) Ace-showing cue-bids.
(4) Not gilt-edged.

Contract: 7◆	**Opening Lead: ♠Q**

Study this Seven Diamond contract - is it a Bridge too far?

You have 12 top tricks, and West's queen of spades lead has told you that he alone guards spades. If he alone guards hearts too, then a squeeze will provide the thirteenth trick. Let us project the ending if you simply played out all your minor-suit winners:

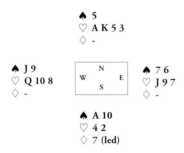

The problem here is that East also guards hearts (hearts is a Weak Threat, guarded by both opponents), enabling West to discard a heart on the final trump (above). No squeeze operates, and you are down one.

You must make sure that only one opponent guards hearts (converting it to a "Strong Threat"), and hope for that opponent to be West. You must *"isolate the guard"*. This can be done (earlier) by playing ace-king and ruffing a heart.

You visualise an ending in which dummy has a heart, the one-card threat (meaning that the Squeeze will only operate from dummy); and your hand has the two-card threat (ace-ten of spades).

Win the king of spades, draw trumps, play ace-king of hearts and ruff a heart (isolating the guard), run your remaining trumps (throwing a spade from dummy on the extra card in hand), then play ace of clubs and a club to the king (in order to be in dummy).

Here is the ending as that second club is led:

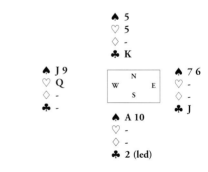

In order to retain the heart, West has to discard the nine of spades (hoping his partner holds the ten). No good - declarer wins dummy's king of clubs, then leads a spade to the ace. West's jack falls and the ten is promoted. 13 tricks and grand slam made.

Deal 27

A Simple Squeeze is one that works on one opponent (as distinct from a Double Squeeze which works on both - see anon). Two suits are normally involved, and one opponent must have sole guard of both.

Take this suit:

```
              North
              Kxxx
      facing  South
              Ax
```

On the likely 4-3 split, both opponents can guard this suit (holding three or more cards). Only if an opponent holds five+ cards will he alone guard the third round of the suit.

However if you play ace-king-ruff a third round, then only one opponent (the one with the four-card length) can guard the suit. You have made a Weak Threat into a Strong Threat; you have "isolated the guard".

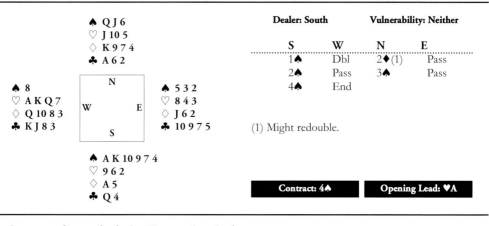

Dealer: South   **Vulnerability: Neither**

S	W	N	E
1♠	Dbl	2♦ (1)	Pass
2♠	Pass	3♠	Pass
4♠	End		

(1) Might redouble.

Contract: 4♠	Opening Lead: ♥A

On our featured deal, West, who had advertised all the missing strength, began with his three top hearts, and then switched safely to his singleton trump (best). As declarer do not waste time reflecting on how to reach the making Three Notrumps. Ask yourself how you can score all the remainder in Four Spades.

You will need a Squeeze. You know (from the bidding) that West guards clubs. You must organise the play so that only he guards diamonds. If he holds five diamonds, he is already the sole guarder of the suit; but if, as is much more likely, he has four diamonds, then you must play ace-king-ruff a diamond to prevent East from co-guarding the suit.

Win the trump switch, draw trumps, then isolate the diamond guard by playing ace-king-ruff a diamond (key plays). Now run your remaining trumps to reach this ending as the last trump is led (see across):

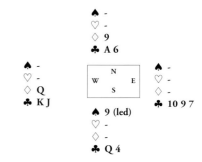

West must throw the jack of clubs in order to retain his diamond guard. Dummy's last diamond can now be thrown - it has served its purpose. You then lead a low club to the (king and) ace, and score the last trick with your promoted queen. 10 tricks and game made.

Deal 28

Many Squeezes occur without you having to do anything special - you may even be unaware of what is happening. You play out all your winners and, hey presto, an opponent looks uncomfortable and you emerge with an extra trick.

However sometimes you need to take specific preparatory measures to bring about a Squeeze. Here are the three most useful techniques (by far):

A) *The Vienna Coup.* Unblocking a winner to make a "split threat" (e.g. ♣Ax facing ♣Qx) into a one-card threat (♣Q).

(B) *Rectifying the Count.* A normal Squeeze requires you to be able to win all the remaining tricks bar one ("N - 1"). If you have, say, all the tricks bar two (N - 2), you must lose a trick before the Squeeze will work.

(C) *Isolating the Guard.* Take a suit of ♠Axxx facing ♠Kx. On a 4-3 split, both opponents guard this suit (on the third round). But if you play king-ace-ruff, then only one opponent can guard it.

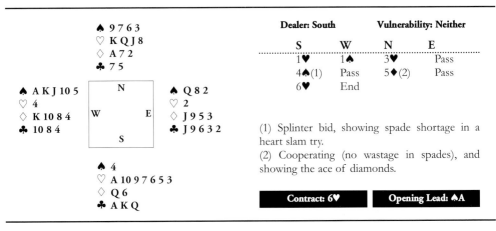

Dealer: South		Vulnerability: Neither	
S	**W**	**N**	**E**
1♥	1♠	3♥	Pass
4♠(1)	Pass	5♦(2)	Pass
6♥	End		

(1) Splinter bid, showing spade shortage in a heart slam try.
(2) Cooperating (no wastage in spades), and showing the ace of diamonds.

Contract: 6♥	**Opening Lead: ♠A**

Six Hearts looks to have a spade and a diamond to lose. Not so - consider that West has advertised five spades, and rates to hold the king of diamonds (East never bid). With West potentially in sole charge of those suits, you can make your slam. But first you must do something to make only West guard spades - see (C) above.

West leads the ace of spades and switches to a trump. You must isolate the spade guard. Win the trump in dummy, ruff a spade, cross to a trump, and ruff a third spade. Now only West guards spades. You lead out all your remaining trumps and clubs to reach this ending as the last trump is led:

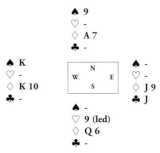

West has to release a diamond in order to keep his spade. But now dummy's spade can be released, whereupon a low diamond to the ace sees West's king pop up. Your promoted queen takes the last trick, and the slam is made.

Deal 29

So far, we have only been squeezing one opponent. But when (almost always) three suits need to be guarded, both opponents can feel the pressure: a Double Squeeze.

Put in layman's terms, if one opponent has sole guard of "Suit A", and the other opponent has sole guard of "Suit B", then neither can guard "Suit C". Typically "A" and "B" will be one-card threats, and "C" will be a two-card threat.

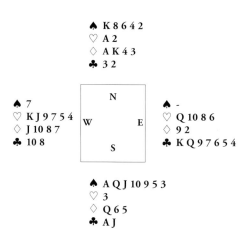

♠ K 8 6 4 2
♡ A 2
◇ A K 4 3
♣ 3 2

♠ 7
♡ K J 9 7 5 4
◇ J 10 8 7
♣ 10 8

♠ -
♡ Q 10 8 6
◇ 9 2
♣ K Q 9 7 6 5 4

♠ A Q J 10 9 5 3
♡ 3
◇ Q 6 5
♣ A J

Dealer: East		Vulnerability: Both	
S	W	N	E
			3♣
4♠	Pass	4NT(1)	Pass
5♠(2)	Pass	5NT(3)	Pass
7♠(4)	End		

(1) Roman Key Card Blackwood (spades).
(2) Two of "five aces" (incl. ♠K); plus ♠Q.
(3) "We have all the keycards - do you fancy a grand slam? If unsure, show me how many side-kings you have".
(4) You may have noticed a trend to overbid in this series. But with all these Squeeze techniques at our fingertips...

Contract: 7♠ | **Opening Lead: ♣10**

Declaring Seven Spades, you win the ten of clubs lead to East's queen, noting that East is marked with the king (and thus in sole charge). You draw trump (note singular), and test diamonds by cashing the three top cards. No easy thirteenth trick - East discards on the third round.

Nil desperandum - far from it. Because East has sole guard of clubs, and West has sole guard of diamonds, neither can guard hearts. Would you believe it that your two of hearts is bound to score the thirteenth trick!

Simply play out all your trumps. You play out your final trump to reach a three-card ending (see across):

West has to discard down to a singleton heart in order to retain the boss diamond. Dummy's diamond can bow be released - it has served its purpose. East, similarly, has to discard down to a singleton heart in order to retain the master

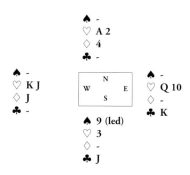

♠ -
♡ A 2
◇ 4
♣ -

♠ -
♡ K J
◇ J
♣ -

♠ -
♡ Q 10
◇ -
♣ K

♠ 9 (led)
♡ 3
◇ -
♣ J

club. You now lead to the ace of hearts, felling the king and queen, and win the last trick with the lowly two of hearts. 13 tricks and grand slam made.

All you had to do was play out all your winners, and watch out for the jack of diamonds and king of clubs. Not too tough!

Deal 30

The basis of the Double Squeeze, that Squeeze on both opponents - is that if one opponent has sole guard of "Suit A", and the other opponent has sole guard of "Suit B", then neither can guard "Suit C". Suits A and B will typically be one-card threats; Suit C, the "Pivot Suit", will be a two-card threat.

The more you familiarise yourself with these endings, the more able you will be to project the play ahead and reach them. Try this:

Here is a standard Double Squeeze:

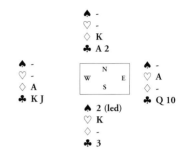

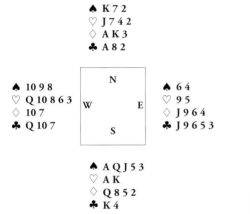

Dealer: North		Vulnerability: Neither	
S	**W**	**N**	**E**
		1♥	Pass
1♠	Pass	1NT	Pass
3♦	Pass	4♠	Pass
4NT(1)	Pass	5♣(2)	Pass
5NT(3)	Pass	6♦(3)	Pass
7♠	End		

(1) Roman Key Card Blackwood (spades).
(2) Zero or three of "five aces" (incl. ♠K).
(3) How many side kings? Answer: one.

Contract: 7♠	Opening Lead: ♠10

You win the trump lead, draw trumps, then try to ruff out the queen of hearts, cashing the ace-king, cross to the king of diamonds, then ruffing a low heart. No queen appears, but West, crucially sitting in front of dummy's jack of hearts threat, holds the guard, enhancing your chances of a Squeeze.

Your other non-Squeeze chance is a 3-3 diamond split, but when you cross to the ace and return to your queen, West discards. No 3-3 split, but you can now say, "West must guard hearts; East must guard diamonds; neither can guard clubs". You play out your last trump to leave a four-card ending (see across):

West has to throw a club to prevent dummy's heart from promoting; the heart is now released. East also has to throw a club, to

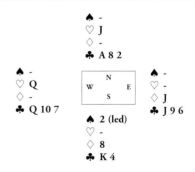

prevent your diamond from being promoted. You cash the king of clubs (throwing dummy's eight for style points), lead over to dummy's ace, and take the last trick with the lowly two of clubs. 13 tricks and grand slam made.

Deal 31

Study this ending and make three tricks (a) with spades as trumps and (b) in notrumps:

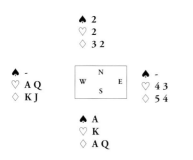

```
          ♠ 2
          ♡ 2
          ◊ 3 2
♠ -                      ♠ -
♡ A Q     W    N    E    ♡ 4 3
◊ K J          S        ◊ 5 4
          ♠ A
          ♡ K
          ◊ A Q
```

(a) With spades as trumps, this is a classic Throw-in. You exit with the king of hearts to West, who must then lead a diamond away from his king, or lead a heart giving you ruff-and-discard, able to throw a diamond from one hand and ruff in the other.

(b) In notrumps, the above strategy is not available. Exit with the heart on this trick and West will win and cash his other heart. But what if you play your spade?

West has no good discard. If he throws the queen of hearts, you will exit with the king of hearts for a forced diamond lead. If he throws the jack of diamonds, then your ace will cash the king. West may discard the ace of hearts, hoping his partner has the king and can win a heart lead. No good here: your king is promoted. West has been "Strip Squeezed".

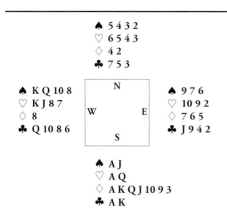

```
              ♠ 5 4 3 2
              ♡ 6 5 4 3
              ◊ 4 2
              ♣ 7 5 3
♠ K Q 10 8         N           ♠ 9 7 6
♡ K J 8 7                      ♡ 10 9 2
◊ 8        W         E         ◊ 7 6 5
♣ Q 10 8 6         S           ♣ J 9 4 2
              ♠ A J
              ♡ A Q
              ◊ A K Q J 10 9 3
              ♣ A K
```

Dealer: South   **Vulnerability: Neither**

S	W	N	E
6◊ (1)	End		

(1) Unsubtle, but the problem with developing the hand via a 2♣ opener is that it will make partner declarer in diamonds after the likely 2◊ negative response. Instead, South surprises all at the table (worth something), and bids the most likely contract.

Contract: 6◊	**Opening Lead: ♠K**

Declarer wins the king of spades lead with the ace and, with no dummy entry to take the heart finesse, paradoxically needs the finesse to be offside (i.e. West holding the king).

Declarer simply runs all his minor-suit cards to leave a four-card ending (see across):

West has no good discard on the final trump. Throw the ten of spades and a spade to his queen will force a heart lead. Throw the jack of hearts and the ace will fell the king. His best chance is to throw the queen spades, hoping his partner holds the jack. No good here though, as declarer's jack is promoted. 12 tricks and slam made.

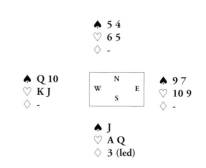

```
              ♠ 5 4
              ♡ 6 5
              ◊ -
♠ Q 10            N           ♠ 9 7
♡ K J                         ♡ 10 9
◊ -        W         E        ◊ -
                  S
              ♠ J
              ♡ A Q
              ◊ 3 (led)
```

Deal 32

A Strip Squeeze (and Throw-in) involves declarer squeezing an opponent down to one-too-few cards, prepared then to throw him in.

We are talking about a doom similar to West's as the ace of clubs is led here:

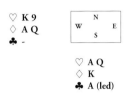

```
    ♡ K 9
    ◇ A Q          N
    ♣ -        W        E
                   S

               ♡ A Q
               ◇ K
               ♣ A (led)
```

A declarer who fancies his ability to read an end-position will rely on the Strip Squeeze more than any other type of endplay. It is very common.

Here is a typical scenario:

(A) Declarer knows the location of the missing high-cards (from the bidding and early play), perhaps rendering a finesse a losing proposition.

(B) Declarer projects ahead to (usually) a three-card ending.

(C) Declarer plays to reach this three-card ending, paying special attention to the defenders cards. For unlike an Elimination and Throw-in or many other Squeezes, the success of the Strip Squeeze depends on declarer's ability to read the cards remaining in the key defender's hand.

```
              ♠ 5 4 3
              ♡ 7 6 5 4 3
              ◇ 8 4 2
              ♣ K 3

♠ Q J 9 8 7      N        ♠ 6 2
♡ A Q 10 8                ♡ J 9 8 7
◇ 6          W       E    ◇ 7 5 3
♣ Q 10 8                  ♣ J 9 7 6 5
                 S
              ♠ A K 10
              ♡ K
              ◇ A K Q J 10 9
              ♣ A 4 2
```

Dealer: West		Vulnerability: Neither	
S	**W**	**N**	**E**
	1♠	Pass	Pass
Dbl	Pass	2♥	Pass
3◆(1)	Pass	4◆	Pass
6◆(2)	End		

(1) Showing a hand too strong to overcall immediately.
(2) A overbid. South needs a perfect club holding opposite even to have a chance.

Contract: 6◆	Opening Lead: ♠Q

Try to visualise the three-card ending on this deal, a slam in which West leads the queen of spades around to your king.

Your last three cards will be ♠A10 and ♥K. Put them on one side, and don't touch them. Instead play out all the other cards. This you do by ruffing a third club, then running all your trumps. What can West discard on the last trump (see across)?

Discard a spade, and the jack will fall under your ace. Discard the queen of hearts, and you will throw him in with the ace to lead away from his spades. Letting go the ace of hearts (good defence, hoping East holds the king) will not work either, as your king is promoted.

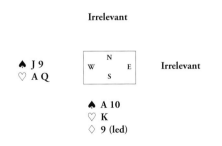

```
♠ J 9            N
♡ A Q        W       E     Irrelevant
                 S
              ♠ A 10
              ♡ K
              ◇ 9 (led)
```

Provided you read the ending, 12 tricks and slam made, making West wish he had led the ace of hearts at Trick One, nullifying any Strip Squeeze.

Deal 33

When you hold the defensive assets and sense that an endplay looms, do not be too predictable.

Study our featured deal, taking the role of West.

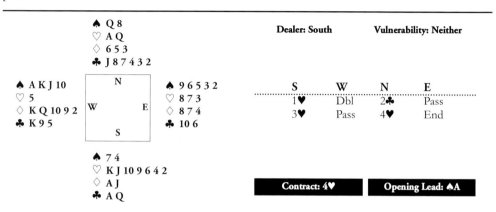

	♠ Q 8		
	♡ A Q		
	◇ 6 5 3		
	♣ J 8 7 4 3 2		

♠ A K J 10　　　　　　　♠ 9 6 5 3 2
♡ 5　　　　　　　　　　♡ 8 7 3
◇ K Q 10 9 2　W　E　◇ 8 7 4
♣ K 9 5　　　　　　　　♣ 10 6

　　　　♠ 7 4
　　　　♡ K J 10 9 6 4 2
　　　　◇ A J
　　　　♣ A Q

Dealer: South　　　**Vulnerability: Neither**

S	W	N	E
1♥	Dbl	2♣	Pass
3♥	Pass	4♥	End

Contract: 4♥　　　**Opening Lead: ♠A**

You cash the ace-king of spades against Four Hearts, then switch to the king of diamonds. Declarer wins the ace, and starts playing trumps (crossing to the ace, and overtaking the queen with the king).

When East shows out on the third trump, you can count declarer with seven trumps. You also know he has no spade left in his hand, or he would surely have trumped it in dummy. Which three cards will you reduce down to, and, also vital, how will you do it? Do your thinking as early as possible, and certainly before the last trump is led.

If you as West do the predictable and come down to these four cards,

Irrelevant

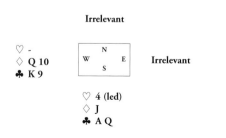

♡ -
◇ Q 10
♣ K 9

♡ 4 (led)
◇ J
♣ A Q

declarer will likely read the ending whatever you discard on the final trump.

Discard the ten of diamonds, and declarer will throw you in with the queen of diamonds to lead away from the king of clubs. An agonised nine of clubs discard will not work either. Declarer will doubtless read your unease, and cash the ace to fell your king. Discarding the queen of diamonds is better technique, and would avert the endplay if your partner holds the jack. Not here though, promoting declarer's jack. In short, you are sunk. Game made.

Much better is to come down to these four cards,

Irrelevant

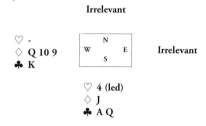

♡ -
◇ Q 10 9
♣ K

♡ 4 (led)
◇ J
♣ A Q

discarding the ten of diamonds on the final trump, to make it appear you have ◆Q and ♣K9 remaining.

An unsuspecting declarer will then exit with the jack of diamonds, expecting you lead into his ace-queen of clubs. He will be disappointed and dismayed when you then cash the nine of diamonds. Down one.

Deal 34

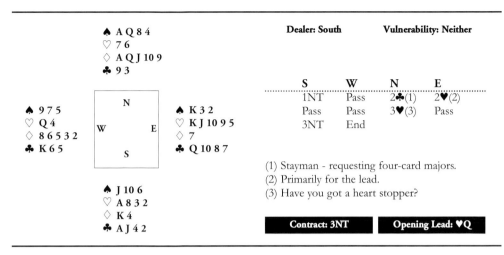

	♠ A Q 8 4		
	♡ 7 6		
	◇ A Q J 10 9		
	♣ 9 3		

Dealer: South   **Vulnerability: Neither**

S	W	N	E
1NT	Pass	2♣(1)	2♥(2)
Pass	Pass	3♥(3)	Pass
3NT	End		

(1) Stayman - requesting four-card majors.
(2) Primarily for the lead.
(3) Have you got a heart stopper?

Contract: 3NT	**Opening Lead: ♥Q**

Declarer viewed West's queen of hearts lead with some consternation. East had overcalled at the Two-Level on a broken suit (which soon turned out to be just five cards in length when West followed twice). This strongly suggested he held the king of spades. With the finesse doomed, declarer had just his eight top tricks.

East overtook the queen of hearts with the king, and, when declarer ducked, continued with the jack. Declarer won the ace this time, knowing that West held no more cards and wanting to retain the third heart as a possible exit card. He planned a Strip Squeeze and Throw-in against East.

Next followed five rounds of diamonds, leaving East to find four discards. The first saw an easy spade; the second a club. There then followed some thought, as East worked out that his partner needed something good in clubs to prevent declarer having nine top tricks. East then discarded two further clubs on the fourth and fifth diamonds.

East's discards were very tell-tale. The easy, early spade, with no further discards of the suit, suggested ♠Kxx; he was known to have ♥KJ109x; he therefore held four clubs - now just one. Can you see what declarer did in the six-card ending (see across).

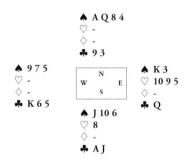

Declarer crossed to his ace of clubs, stripping East of his safe exit, then led a heart. East could win his three hearts, but at Trick 12 had to lead a spade around to the ace-queen. Nine tricks made.

Though declarer can always succeed if he reads it, East would have done better to have discarded two painless spades, feigning ♠Kxxx. Unless declarer dropped the singleton king, he would now fail - with East having too many winners after being thrown in.

Remember that - a smooth baring of a king will normally be the best defence to a Strip Squeeze.

Deal 35

Many contracts are allowed to make by poor discarding, which is the best reason to run a long suit in notrumps.

However sometimes there is simply nothing a defender can do:

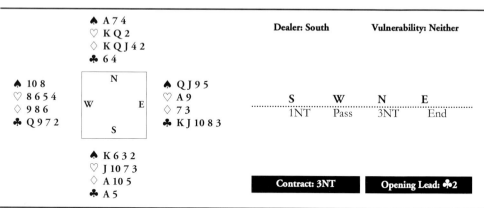

	♠ A 7 4	
	♡ K Q 2	
	◇ K Q J 4 2	
	♣ 6 4	

♠ 10 8	N	♠ Q J 9 5
♡ 8 6 5 4	W E	♡ A 9
◇ 9 8 6		◇ 7 3
♣ Q 9 7 2	S	♣ K J 10 8 3

	♠ K 6 3 2	
	♡ J 10 7 3	
	◇ A 10 5	
	♣ A 5	

Dealer: South **Vulnerability: Neither**

S	W	N	E
1NT	Pass	3NT	End

Contract: 3NT **Opening Lead: ♣2**

Simply win West's two of clubs lead (marking him with four cards, and thus East with five) with the ace (first or second round - say second), and run five rounds of diamonds. East can painlessly discard a spade and a heart, but what does he discard on the fifth (see across):

A spade discard sees declarer make long cards in the suit; need I say anything about the ace of hearts; and a club enables declarer to knock out the ace of hearts - as the defenders now have insufficient club winners to cash. In practice East should discard a spade, in the hope that his

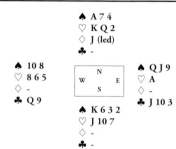

	♠ A 7 4	
	♡ K Q 2	
	◇ J (led)	
	♣ -	

♠ 10 8	N	♠ Q J 9
♡ 8 6 5	W E	♡ A
◇ -	S	◇ -
♣ Q 9		♣ J 10 3

	♠ K 6 3 2	
	♡ J 10 7	
	◇ -	
	♣ -	

partner can guard the suit, but that doesn't work here. Game made (plus one on a spade discard).

Let's see another of this type of three-suit pressure-on-a-long-suit:

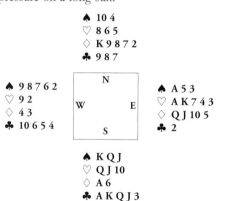

	♠ 10 4	
	♡ 8 6 5	
	◇ K 9 8 7 2	
	♣ 9 8 7	

♠ 9 8 7 6 2	N	♠ A 5 3
♡ 9 2	W E	♡ A K 7 4 3
◇ 4 3	S	◇ Q J 10 5
♣ 10 6 5 4		♣ 2

	♠ K Q J	
	♡ Q J 10	
	◇ A 6	
	♣ A K Q J 3	

Declaring Three Notrumps after East has opened One Heart, the defence play ace-king and a third heart. You appear to have just eight tricks, but try running clubs.

East can afford two spades and a diamond, but his whole hand collapses on the fifth club. This is because he has sole guard of both spades and diamonds (the key ingredients for such a Squeeze to operate). East may well release a heart to retain these guards, but now you knock out the ace of spades, knowing East has just one heart to cash. Game made.

Deal 36

Consider the following position:

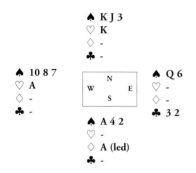

```
            ♠ K J 3
            ♡ K
            ◇ -
            ♣ -
  ♠ 10 8 7         ♠ Q 6
  ♡ A      N       ♡ -
  ◇ -    W   E     ◇ -
  ♣ -      S       ♣ 3 2
            ♠ A 4 2
            ♡ -
            ◇ A (led)
            ♣ -
```

You lead the winning diamond, forcing West, known to have the ace of hearts, to discard a spade. You throw dummy's king of hearts, and must now play spades. You cash the ace and lead over to dummy's king-jack. West plays low a second time, and you must decide whether or not to finesse.

Don't! West cannot hold the queen of spades because his last card is known to be the ace of hearts. Even if you have lost count of spades, you know it cannot be right to finesse. You rise with the ace and, lo and behold, East's queen comes tumbling down.

This is known as a Show-up Squeeze ("Pop up" in the States), because if West (above) holds the queen it will show up. If it doesn't, then East must have the queen.

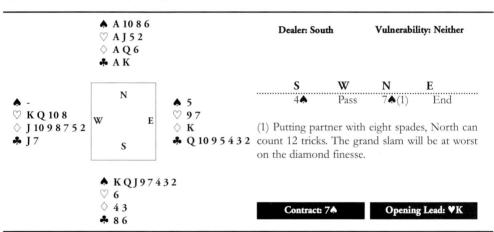

```
              ♠ A 10 8 6
              ♡ A J 5 2
              ◇ A Q 6
              ♣ A K
  ♠ -                     ♠ 5
  ♡ K Q 10 8      N       ♡ 9 7
  ◇ J 10 9 8 7 5 2  W   E  ◇ K
  ♣ J 7             S      ♣ Q 10 9 5 4 3 2
              ♠ K Q J 9 7 4 3 2
              ♡ 6
              ◇ 4 3
              ♣ 8 6
```

Dealer: South   Vulnerability: Neither

S	W	N	E
4♠	Pass	7♠(1)	End

(1) Putting partner with eight spades, North can count 12 tricks. The grand slam will be at worst on the diamond finesse.

| **Contract: 7♠** | **Opening Lead: ♥K** |

Declaring Seven Spades on the king of hearts lead, you appear to need the queen of hearts (marked with West) to ruff out in three rounds with (more likely) a diamond finesse to fall back upon.

Winning the ace of hearts, you draw trump (note singular), ruff a heart, cross to a club, and ruff a third heart. West's queen has not fallen, and you are pretty much resigned to the diamond finesse.

Or are you? Cash dummy's other club, and run your trumps. As you lead your last trump, West must discard a diamond in order to retain the boss heart. Dummy's jack of hearts is now discarded, but its presence has (crucially) forced West to reduce to one diamond.

When you lead a diamond to dummy's ace-queen at Trick 12 and West plays low, you know that East holds the king, for West's last card is the queen of hearts. There is no point in finessing. You rise with the ace and the king is felled. 13 tricks and grand slam made.

You would know the king would fall if you had counted all the diamonds. But you did not need to keep count to succeed (good!), and I think of my old Maths teacher "Jakes", who used to say "never do any work unless you have to".

Deal 37

Have a look at the this ending:

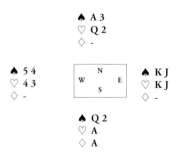

The blockage appears to make winning all four tricks impossible, but try the effect of leading the ace of diamonds and discarding dummy's small spade. East is "Criss-Cross Squeezed" (the term used to describe such a blocked-position Squeeze).

If East discards the jack of spades, you cross to the ace of spades, return to the ace of hearts, then cash the promoted queen of spades. And if he lets go the jack of hearts, you cash the ace of hearts felling his king, cross to the ace of spades, and cash the promoted queen of hearts.

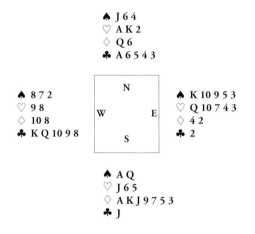

Dealer: South   **Vulnerability: North - South**

S	W	N	E
1◇	Pass	2♣	2◇ (1)
3◇	Pass	4NT(2)	Pass
5♣(3)	Pass	5NT(4)	Pass
7◇(5)	End		

(1) Michaels - showing five-five in majors.
(2) Roman Key Card Blackwood (diamonds).
(3) Zero or three of "five aces" (incl. ◆K).
(4) Confirming all the key cards are present, and inviting a grand. If South can't decide, then he shows his number of side-kings.
(4) Based on the seventh trump and likely-working spade finesse.

Contract: 7◆	**Opening Lead: ♣K**

Win the ace of clubs and ruff a club, East who has advertised ten major-suit cards, unsurprisingly discarding. Now run off all your trumps. When you lead the last trump (see across), and discard dummy's two of hearts, East is "criss-crossed".

If East discards a heart, you cross to the ace-king of hearts felling his queen, lead a spade to your queen, and cash the ace of spades and promoted jack of hearts. A spade discard from East works no better either: you cross to the king of hearts, finesse the queen of spades, cash the ace felling his king, then return to the ace of hearts to cash the promoted jack of spades. 13 tricks and grand slam made.

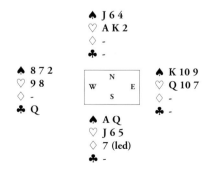

Deal 38

Have a look at Position A (across), needing all six tricks with hearts trumps.

Play ace-king-ruff a club (isolating the guard), then play your final trump. West is caught in a Positional Squeeze. Can you also win if East holds the guards (see Position B)?

You cannot succeed by the above route, but how about cashing your penultimate trump throwing dummy's small diamond? If East discards a diamond, you cross to dummy's ace felling his king, then ace-king-ruff a club and cash the promoted diamond. If East discards a club, then ace-king-ruff a club will set up the long card with the ace of diamonds as an entry.

East is victim of a "Trump Squeeze", named as such because the technique integrally involves ruffing out a suit after the Squeeze has operated (on the penultimate trump). The expert loves the Trump Squeeze because you can win when guards are sitting over threats; however, like the similar Criss-Cross, you have to read the ending.

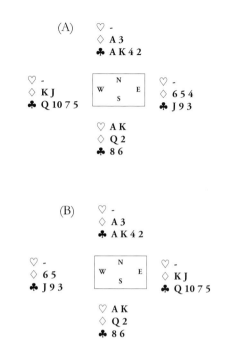

(A)
```
              ♡ -
              ◇ A 3
              ♣ A K 4 2
♡ -                        ♡ -
◇ K J          N           ◇ 6 5 4
♣ Q 10 7 5   W   E         ♣ J 9 3
                 S
              ♡ A K
              ◇ Q 2
              ♣ 8 6
```

(B)
```
              ♡ -
              ◇ A 3
              ♣ A K 4 2
♡ -                        ♡ -
◇ 6 5          N           ◇ K J
♣ J 9 3      W   E         ♣ Q 10 7 5
                 S
              ♡ A K
              ◇ Q 2
              ♣ 8 6
```

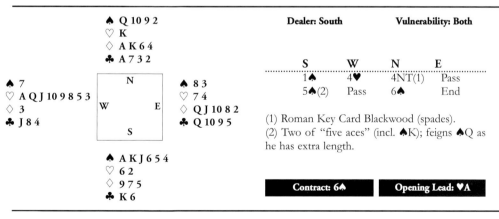

```
              ♠ Q 10 9 2
              ♡ K
              ◇ A K 6 4
              ♣ A 7 3 2
♠ 7                          ♠ 8 3
♡ A Q J 10 9 8 5 3   N       ♡ 7 4
◇ 3                W   E     ◇ Q J 10 8 2
♣ J 8 4                      ♣ Q 10 9 5
                     S
              ♠ A K J 6 5 4
              ♡ 6 2
              ◇ 9 7 5
              ♣ K 6
```

Dealer: South **Vulnerability: Both**

S	W	N	E
1♠	4♥	4NT(1)	Pass
5♠(2)	Pass	6♠	End

(1) Roman Key Card Blackwood (spades).
(2) Two of "five aces" (incl. ♠K); feigns ♠Q as he has extra length.

Contract: 6♠	Opening Lead: ♥A

West cashes the ace of hearts and switches passively to a diamond. Win the king, cross to a trump, ruff a heart, then lead out trumps.

Look at the ending as the penultimate trump is led, dummy's diamond being discarded:

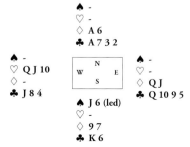

```
              ♠ -
              ♡ -
              ◇ A 6
              ♣ A 7 3 2
♠ -                          ♠ -
♡ Q J 10         N           ♡ -
◇ -            W   E         ◇ Q J
♣ J 8 4                      ♣ Q 10 9 5
                 S
              ♠ J 6 (led)
              ♡ -
              ◇ 9 7
              ♣ K 6
```

East is Trump Squeezed. A diamond promotes your small diamond. A club enables you to play ace-king-ruff a club and set up a long card. 12 tricks and slam made.

Deal 39

Our final weird and wonderful ending (our last deal will see us recap the book) is the Overtaking Trump Squeeze. Make all four tricks with South on lead and clubs trumps here:

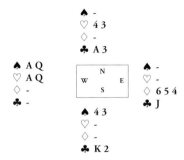

A Crossruff does not work as East overruffs dummy small trump. The only winning line is to lead the king of trumps, putting West in the spotlight.

If West discards a spade, you play low from dummy, so that you retain the lead and can ruff a spade to set up your long card. You then ruff a heart back to hand and cash the spade. If West discards a heart, you overtake the king of trumps with the ace, and ruff a heart to set up a long heart, ruffing a spade to return to the promoted heart. Truly ingenious - and it happens too (occasionally)!

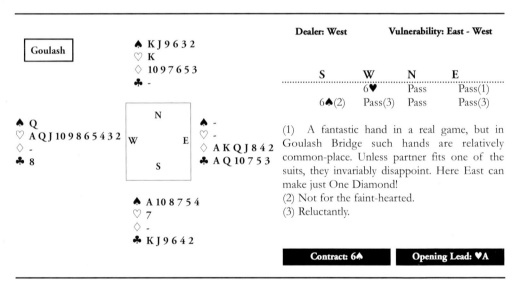

Dealer: West   **Vulnerability: East - West**

S	W	N	E
	6♥	Pass	Pass(1)
6♠(2)	Pass(3)	Pass	Pass(3)

(1) A fantastic hand in a real game, but in Goulash Bridge such hands are relatively common-place. Unless partner fits one of the suits, they invariably disappoint. Here East can make just One Diamond!
(2) Not for the faint-hearted.
(3) Reluctantly.

| Contract: 6♠ | Opening Lead: ♥A |

Take this slam deal (I admit - a "ghoulie", with cards dealt in clumps of five-five-three). West's ace of hearts cashed (I bet that surprised him), East discarding a diamond, and at Trick Two West switched to his singleton queen of trumps (not obvious, but a club switch would have beaten the slam). Over to you.

A trick short (with 11 trump winners), you need a long card from either minor. The key is to force East to commit before you. Your big moment occurs now.

You must cover the queen of trumps with dummy's king, awaiting East's discard. If he throws a diamond, you let the king win, and can now ruff five diamonds to set up the sixth; if East throws a club, you overtake the king of trumps with the ace, and can set up the sixth club, ruffing five times.

A lovely overtaking position, I'm sure you will agree, which would not have been possible if the ace and king of trumps were swapped.